CAREERS IN

NONPROFIT ORGANIZATION MANAGEMENT

IF WORKING FOR THE PUBLIC GOOD appeals to you, there may be a management level job waiting for you at one of the more than 1.5 million nonprofit organizations based in the United States. Working at a nonprofit organization is not just a job, it is a mission, in some cases even a calling. When you are part of a management team at a nonprofit, you have a chance to make a positive difference in people's lives every day. In the nonprofit world it is not about how much money your organization made today. The measure of your success is how many people you helped today. If you solved someone's problem, eased someone's pain, you had a good day.

When you hold a management position at a nonprofit, you are responsible for guiding the organization and its employees to ensure its mission is accomplished. Whether the aim is aiding individuals or society as a whole, it all comes down to making the world a better place. Not all nonprofits are about social work. Many focus on advocacy, protecting animal rights, safeguarding the environment, fighting for benefits for members and veterans of the armed forces, keeping parkland pristine, supporting the arts, and leading the charge for social change. Also included in the nonprofit sector are religious institutions, trade associations, and private foundations dedicated to awarding grants to worthy recipients. These stand alongside nonprofit organizations devoted to research, education, and job training.

Oftentimes the voice for the voiceless, nonprofits bring issues to the fore that would otherwise be overlooked. There are thousands of issues and worthy causes championed by nonprofits. One of the allures of going into the nonprofit field is the wide variety of organizations where you can work.

Management positions include executive and assistant executive director, as well as directors of departments like fundraising, community outreach, media relations, volunteers, and special events. This is important work that goes way beyond a nine-to-five job. When you are on staff at a nonprofit, especially in management, your work is never done. There is always another goal to strive for. That is what makes it both challenging and rewarding. There is a teamwork atmosphere because the people who work there and the volunteers who freely give of their time are so committed to the cause.

If you want to roll up your sleeves and be on the front lines in the fight to end social ills and leave the world in a better place, a nonprofit management job should be at the top of your list of career choices.

WHAT YOU CAN DO NOW

THE BEST WAY TO FIND OUT IF NONPROFIT WORK is for you is to try it out. Fortunately, there is no nonprofit that would not benefit from the assistance of an eager volunteer like you. To learn the ropes, volunteer at a nonprofit in a field you might like to go into. For example, if you are interested in the environment and advocacy work, you might want to volunteer at an organization like a local chapter of the Sierra Club. Volunteer for a job in a department you hope to manage as a professional in the nonprofit field, like fundraising or community outreach. Take the time to learn about the entire operation and see if you can shadow the executive director to get a good overview of how the nonprofit operates.

Though the work at various nonprofits might be similar – such as managing volunteers, handling community outreach, doing public relations, and raising funds – there are differences in management style. It is a good idea to volunteer at more than one nonprofit organization. You might want to spend several summers doing this, dividing your time between a big and a small nonprofit, and noting the differences between the two. Do not hesitate to ask questions about the policies and approaches the nonprofit takes to particular issues. The answers might surprise you and can be informative for someone aspiring to work in management in the nonprofit field.

HISTORY OF THE FIELD

THE IDEA OF HELPING THE LESS FORTUNATE and volunteering for the common good dates back thousands of years in Europe and to Colonial times in America. Religious organizations have been in the vanguard of charitable causes throughout human history. The church took on the responsibility of helping the disadvantaged in Medieval Europe. Townspeople and neighbors would also get together and form loosely knit organizations that would help the poor, the sick, or those who had fallen on hard times.

Government got involved in 1601 when the British Parliament passed the Charitable Uses Act. The measure set forth a list of causes the British government felt benefited society, and called on people to consider donating money to those causes whenever they could, even in their wills.

In Colonial America, people were all too aware of the harsh times that could befall those trying to put down roots in a new land, and when the need arose, settlers would band together and help the downtrodden. In Colonial days, if a road had to be repaired, a group of neighbors would get together, buy supplies, and do the job. The same was true if the local church or meetinghouse needed fixing up.

A young Benjamin Franklin brought back from London an interesting idea in 1726. Franklin went to England to sharpen his skills as a printer. While doing that, he saw all the voluntary organizations being set up by tradespeople in England to protect their interests and help each other advance in their field. Upon his return to the Colonies, Franklin started Junto, a group of young Philadelphia tradespeople and artisans who exchanged ideas and helped each other professionally. Franklin's group laid the groundwork for a number of similar groups and is considered a forerunner of many of today's nonprofit business groups and associations.

The US Civil War prompted the formation of charitable and volunteer groups in both the North and the South. Members gathered supplies for the war effort, helped in hospitals, raised money for their side of the conflict, and rallied men to join the military. Volunteers usually ran these organizations.

Another boost to the concept of nonprofit-style organizations came in the late 1800s when steel magnate Andrew Carnegie started distributing his wealth to start and support museums, libraries, the arts, and education. He also hired management personnel to run these endeavors. Other industrialists, like John D. Rockefeller and

Henry Ford, soon followed.

The tax laws helped clarify the status of nonprofits in the United States. The Revenue Act of 1894 was extremely beneficial to nonprofits because the law made charitable, educational, and religious organizations tax exempt. The tax-exempt status was soon granted to other forms of nonprofit organizations as well. The rationale behind making nonprofits tax exempt was that they were serving the public good, even stepping in to help people when the government was unable to or simply did not have the resources. The Revenue Act of 1894 made it clear that, for an organization to be considered nonprofit and therefore tax exempt, no part of the income of the organization could benefit any individual or private stockholder. That concept is still used to define a nonprofit group today.

In the Revenue Act of 1917, Congress gave taxpayers a federal income tax deduction if they donated money to a tax-exempt organization. Legislators hoped the tax break would encourage people to contribute money to the growing number of nonprofits that were addressing social ills in the nation. The law did increase donations to these organizations and led Congress to pass a law a year later making bequests federally tax deductible as well.

In 1954, the modern federal tax code was established, including section 501C, which covers tax-exempt organizations. Today 501C lists 29 different types of nonprofit organizations. As the federal tax code was revised, more nonprofit organizations came in existence. There was a slight boom in the early 1950s, and then a big increase came in the 1970s.

People began to realize that government, on any level, could not address many of the social problems facing the nation. Chief among those problems were funding research for curing serious illnesses, like cancer and heart disease, advocating to protect animals, cleaning up the environment, promoting literacy, feeding the hungry, housing the homeless, maintaining woodlands and natural streams, safeguarding historic sites, and a whole host of other causes.

Nonprofits targeting these issues had to be managed efficiently and effectively by professionals who could oversee all aspects of the organization and show results. Though they are not businesses, nonprofits need to be run by people with business savvy and skills. Money has to be accounted for and programs have to achieve their goals as well as meet the needs of those being served.

Professionals in the business world started seeing how they could impact nonprofits and began trading in luxury offices for desks at organizations where they could effect change and make the world a better place. Nonprofits were driven by a mission and a management team determined to accomplish that mission. Since the 1970s, hardworking advocates have joined together to start nonprofit organizations to address various important issues that have come to the fore, like wounded US military veterans, that would otherwise be overlooked.

WHERE YOU WILL WORK

THE NONPROFIT SECTOR IS EXTREMELY DIVERSE. Do not just think of a nonprofit as a homeless shelter or a legal aid office, though organizations that provide those kinds of direct services play a big part. In addition to social service agencies, the umbrella of nonprofits also covers organizations involved with advocacy, research, environmental conservation, education, healthcare, animal welfare, arts, and culture, as well as faith-based groups, trade associations, and private foundations.

The focus, clientele, problems, and missions of nonprofits vary, but they exist everywhere. Nonprofits abound in rural and suburban areas as well as in cities. Managers are employed to run different aspects of these organizations, as well as the organizations as a whole. Nonprofits can be located in a cramped basement office in an urban commercial building or a spacious suite in a big, modern, suburban office complex, depending on what the organization can afford and what will best serve the cause it promotes. For instance, a nonprofit distributing food to the needy would most likely reach more people by being headquartered in a storefront in the community it serves.

You could be running a national nonprofit, like the American Heart Association, which has a huge budget and offices and volunteers across the nation. You might be the executive director of a local charity, which operates on a shoestring budget, serving people in one particular neighborhood.

Even though you are in management, you do not sit behind a desk when you work for a social-service nonprofit – at least not all the time. The community becomes your extended office. You get out among the people the nonprofit serves, overseeing that the organization's goals are being met. Depending on the nonprofit's mission, you are making sure toys are being given out to children during the holidays, coats are being distributed to disadvantaged people, heating fuel is being supplied during the winter, medical clinics are properly staffed, and homes damaged by a natural disaster are being repaired.

At an advocacy group, like an environmental or civil rights group, besides your work in the organization's headquarters, you spend a great deal of time in Washington, DC and in state capitals around the country, working to get the support of elected officials for important legislation to help your nonprofit's mission.

Trade associations, like the American Association of Advertising Agencies and the Professional Photographers of America, want you to meet with the membership and giants in the industry, as well as attending trade conferences. Trade associations offer a variety of services to their members, including training, continuing education, job boards, news in the industry, advocacy, and networking. You have to be ahead of the curve by knowing the latest trends in the industry and what the association's members need and want.

Foundations make grants to other nonprofits. Spending time at each nonprofit that applies for a grant from the foundation you are in charge of, will take up part of your time. You want to make sure that the money given out by your foundation goes to organizations that work within your guidelines and that the money is being used properly.

THE WORK YOU WILL DO

THE NONPROFIT WORLD OPERATES ON A pretty straightforward formula: The success or failure of the organization rests with the management team. Having a good cause simply is not enough to be successful; neither is hard work alone. It takes strong, knowledgeable, and decisive leadership. Management sets the course, devises strategy, and runs a well-organized machine.

Nonprofits are designed to grow and help more people and serve an even larger community. With 1.5 million nonprofits in the United States, your organization has to stand out to get its share of grants, donations, and volunteers. Giving the organization a presence and stature in the public eye is one of the many responsibilities of a nonprofit's management team.

Just how large the management team is depends on the size of the nonprofit. The smaller the nonprofit, the more responsibility the executive director shoulders alone, wearing many hats in that leadership role. Roughly 75 percent of all nonprofits in the United States are small, with budgets under $1 million a year. It is not unusual to find executive directors of these small nonprofits running the overall operation, as well as heading up the fundraising, volunteer recruitment, and marketing efforts of the organization. The executive director might have some paid help, but whoever else is on the management team is most likely also handling several jobs.

Mid-sized and big nonprofits have much larger management teams than smaller nonprofits, and that gives those organizations the leeway to have specialists manage individual departments, like fundraising, public relations, volunteers, community outreach, programs, and advocacy. The executive director oversees and must approve everything that goes on at the nonprofit, regardless of the size of the organization.

Executive Director

One of the major aspects of an executive director's job is planning. Most nonprofits do not have the money or personnel to waste on a poorly planned event, program, or campaign. Executive directors have to put together a master plan for the calendar and the fiscal year. No details or expenses can be overlooked. If a nonprofit falls short of its goals, that might require reductions in programs and staff layoffs.

At a nonprofit, everything works together. If a nonprofit wants to serve a certain number of people in the community, the organization will need to raise the funds to accomplish that goal. In crafting the organization's fundraising drive, that goal is always paramount, as is building public support for the cause. If the nonprofit reaches its goal and serves the number of people it intended to, it can increase the number of people it wants to reach the next year and set higher goals for its fundraising campaign.

Specifying the details of how the fundraising effort will be carried out is the director's job. Executive directors work to boost fundraising campaigns every year, coming up with ideas to expand their organization's donor base or working with the group's fundraising director to develop new and exciting ways to encourage people to donate to the nonprofit. One important part of that plan is to constantly give existing donors updates on how their contributions are being used. In their leadership role, executive directors make sure donors are kept abreast of what is going on at the organization.

Networking is crucial to an executive director's job. Executive directors should be highly visible members of the community. They should know corporate leaders, elected officials, religious leaders, prominent citizens, and management personnel at other nonprofits. All these people can help the executive director accomplish the mission of the organization.

A board of directors governs a nonprofit. Executive directors must work closely with their board of directors in order for a nonprofit to run smoothly. Skilled executive directors get the most out of their relationship with their board, building a dialogue with them and cultivating a sense of trust.

A nonprofit's board of directors has oversight over the organization's activities. Boards often vote on key issues facing the organization. The best board decisions are made by people who know all the ins and out of an issue. The executive director gives board members insight into these issues, answers their questions, and lets them know how to steer the organization smoothly into the future. Members of the board are volunteers who care about the nonprofit and want it to succeed. They are natural allies of the management team. Board members can bring in donations, help market the organization, and volunteer their time at events. Members of a nonprofit's board come from various backgrounds and bring an array of talents to the organization, including business skills. This is just the type of know-how a smart executive director can put to work.

A successful executive director builds and retains a loyal workforce. That means encouraging teamwork, involving employees in decision-making, knowing when to give a pat on the back and when to grant employees greater responsibility. A leader of any nonprofit has to make sure its employees and volunteers believe in the organization's mission.

Keeping everyone focused on the mission is not an easy task. People cannot get too excited when things are running smoothly or too down when things are not going so well. Strong leaders strive to inspire their staff and volunteers, so they never lose sight of the big prize – reaching the goals of the organization.

Executive directors cannot afford to be out of touch with the people their organization serves. Whether your organization is providing direct services or doing advocacy work, as the executive director you have to know what is going on in the field. Being on the front lines with employees and volunteers is essential.

Director of Volunteers

A director of volunteers is right in the middle of the fray. Directors of volunteers are very hands-on, always on the lookout for new volunteers and, when those people come onboard, training them for the task ahead. Even after volunteers are trained, it is up to the director of volunteers to supervise those workers, making sure every job is completed correctly.

Most important is maintaining volunteer interest. Volunteers have to understand how vital the work they are doing is. Since they are working for free, volunteers also have to enjoy what they are doing and find it rewarding and gratifying. They must feel valued and appreciated. The director of volunteers is in charge of recognizing the work these individuals do and is responsible for energizing the volunteer corps. Most nonprofits simply could not function without a committed group of volunteers.

Program Director

A nonprofit's programs are often run with the help of volunteers. So program directors and volunteer directors usually work very closely together. Some programs operate every day, others only occasionally. Some are annual or semi-annual events.

Programs may vary from direct services for people in need, like serving dinners at a soup kitchen or distributing food at a food pantry, to promoting the cause by distributing literature about the organization at a county fair or a street festival. Each program – no matter how large or small – has to be coordinated. It is up to the director of programs to assemble the materials for every program and to assign the right number of staff members and volunteers needed to make that program a success.

The director of programs makes suggestions about how programs can be improved or updated to meet more pressing needs, and comes up with ideas for new programs as well. This job requires top-notch organizational skills and the person in this job has to have the ability to plan and run multiple programs at the same time.

Public Relations and Community Outreach

Public relations, marketing, and community outreach can be done by one person or, in large nonprofits, by individual directors of each of those departments working together. These jobs are essential because they keep a nonprofit in the public eye.

Community outreach is about rolling up your sleeves, getting out into the field, and generating support for your mission. You educate people about the cause and what you are doing to address the needs of the community. Part of the job involves speaking before local civic groups. People might think they know what your organization is all about, but your nonprofit often offers programs that the public is unaware of.

For example, people may know that your organization provides hot meals at a soup kitchen. However, they might not know that your program serves breakfast, lunch, and dinner. They may not realize that your organization has volunteers who deliver meals to shut-ins. People might not be aware that local chefs volunteer on different days once a week to cook the meals your organization serves.

Once you get this information out to the public, more people might want to make donations or volunteer to participate in your nonprofit's programs. Supermarkets might offer to donate food, more chefs might come forward to volunteer, and corporations might want to get their employees involved in the work your organization does or contribute money.

Public relations directors deal with the news media. When print, broadcast, or online media cover the activities of a nonprofit, the organization spreads its message to a vast audience. Keeping your organization in the news is an excellent way to develop name recognition and create a following. It also gives the nonprofit an aura of legitimacy. Part of the job of the public relations director is to stay in touch with donors, volunteers, and members through newsletters, emails, and social media.

Marketing directors promote a nonprofit's brand. As the director of marketing, your goal is to have people see the name and logo of the nonprofit you work for everywhere they turn. So you place posters at bus stops, train stations, and supermarkets; plaster billboards on highways; write, record, and air public service announcements on radio and television; put notices in community theater programs; insert brochures about the organization in public information areas at the local library and at city hall; and hand out trinkets with the group's name and logo on them at public events.

Fundraising Director

Fundraising directors raise the money needed to keep a nonprofit in operation. Today, for most nonprofits, small and large, attracting contributions is a year-round endeavor. The one-time annual fundraising drive has turned into an ongoing effort to sustain a steady cash flow. That calls for identifying your donor base and encouraging people to contribute as much and as often as they can. Fundraising directors are always looking for new sources of revenue and developing new avenues to attract donations, like auctions, fashion shows, runs, festivals, cooking contests, dinners, celebrity book signings – anything that might be fun and bring in some money.

Advocacy Director

Nonprofits fighting for a cause often try to bring about social change. Many nonprofits have an advocacy director charged with overseeing the organization's efforts to change public policy through legislation, education, and by raising public awareness of the issues the nonprofit addresses. Advocacy is usually done on a grassroots level, with people signing petitions, writing letters and emails to elected officials, speaking up at public meetings, attending rallies, and calling attention to the issue any way they can.

Advocacy efforts require an effective leader who organizes the campaign and makes sure it conforms to a nonprofit's mission and philosophy. For instance, a nonprofit that focuses on environmental protection may hold a rally at a park to call attention to maintaining as much open space as possible. The organization would want to make sure the park was left as it was found, with no garbage strewn around and no damage to the grassland or foliage.

Nonprofits, especially large ones, add directors for departments they specifically need, such as finance, membership, and special events.

NONPROFIT MANAGERS TELL ABOUT THEIR CAREERS

I Am the Executive Director of a Small Nonprofit

"I think we are the typical small nonprofit with a limited staff of six full-time employees and four part-time people, a very tight budget, and an important mission. I like running a nonprofit of this size because you get a chance to be involved in every aspect of the operation.

Though there is a paid staff member to handle fundraising, I am also very much involved in that function. The fundraising director helps with our volunteers and public relations efforts as well. No matter what your job title is, when you work at a small nonprofit you are basically involved in helping to run every aspect of the organization. We go out in the community we serve all the time and meet with the people who turn to us for help. We learn about where we are making inroads and where we have to do better. In a small nonprofit, you never lose touch with your mission and the people you are serving.

We have some very dedicated volunteers. We could not get the job done without our volunteers. While we need money to keep our doors open, the work these volunteers do almost means more than monetary contributions. Part of my job is letting these volunteers know how much they mean to this organization, and that they are valued and appreciated. I also try to encourage them to bring more volunteers into the group.

In a small nonprofit, volunteers can never be overlooked or treated like a number, or as if they don't really belong because they are not a paid staff member. You have to know the names of all the volunteers and what they are good at, and put them in jobs where they really feel they are making a contribution. You can't have volunteers come here and stand around. They want to make a contribution, and you need them to do something meaningful, so you have to plan well and make good use of the time these volunteers are giving.

Networking is very important for a small nonprofit. We are not going to get the type of contributions a big national nonprofit is going to get, but that doesn't mean we have to be satisfied with small donations. I network with businesspeople in our area and get community leaders to understand what we do and the important needs we fulfill.

For instance, we provide people in need in the community with food – packaged goods mostly. Almost any business can help us by doing a food drive, and there are some stores in the area that help by donating some dry goods to us. These businesses might not realize what they can do to help us. It's my job to make every business think of us when they want to do something to help the community.

Every time a company runs a successful food drive for us that means we don't have to buy the food ourselves. We can then use that money later on when the shelves are empty and we don't have a food drive to fall back on.

I don't think there is a better way to learn how to stretch a budget, get the most from your staff, and involve community resources in your mission than to work for a small nonprofit. I certainly think you learn the most important lesson of all about nonprofits when you work at a small nonprofit, and that's teamwork."

I Am the Director of Fundraising at a Regional Nonprofit

"Today, more than ever before, fundraising is one of the most important aspects of any nonprofit. It is the determining factor in whether your organization can continue to exist. We count more on private donations than on government grants or even corporate support.

There is a great deal of competition for donor dollars. One of the first things you have to do is identify your donor base and then go after that base. I found one of the best ways to do this is through networking. This is where you have to rely on your organization's board members, volunteers, even vendors – anyone who has anything to do with your organization. Ask these people to introduce you to their social network, anyone they know who might have an interest in the cause or might want to support the organization, even with a small donation. Then you have to piggyback off those introductions and get those people to introduce you to their social network and so forth. Just keep going, meeting more and more people.

I'm a bit old fashioned about this but I think it's essential to meet these people in person. I think this is the best way to build a fundraising constituency. You can buy donor lists, but I think being introduced person-to-person works so much better. You establish a certain trust right off the bat.

You have to be able to sell your organization. Chances are these people have made donations to other organizations that support a similar cause or mission. Without downplaying any other nonprofit, you have to talk up your organization and its accomplishments in order to gain someone's support. So you have to give them reasons. Get them to come to your events. Invite them to see your organization in action. Have them meet some of the people you have helped or see how the organization has made a difference in the community.

Getting donors who will make a sizable gift takes a personal touch. You have to show an interest in them so they will eventually take an interest in you. I want to get potential donors involved in the organization, make them believers in what the group has done and can continue to do. I want them to feel as though they have a stake in what we are doing and can take pride in our accomplishments.

Your job does not end once you get a donor. You have to work just as hard to keep those donors in the fold. You want donations from them at least every year. That means keeping donors informed about how their money is being spent and what you have accomplished lately. To do that you have to know your donors. Some like to be contacted with updates on a regular basis; others find that once or twice a year is sufficient. Some respond to getting information through the regular mail; others by phone or social media. It's your job to know which donors respond best to each type of contact.

It's always good to keep your website updated. To most donors, old news is no news. When a website is not updated, it's as if you aren't doing anything new and that always hurts donations.

Another tip: I've always felt every donor should know that he or she is appreciated, every donation valued. So if you're at an event and see a donor there, take the time to thank that person by name. You'll get another donation from that person soon – I guarantee it."

I Am the Executive Director of a National Trade Association

"Trade associations are usually made up of dues-paying members who are professionals in a particular industry, like moving and storage, booksellers, home furnishings, photography, and so on. We are nonprofit and our way of bettering society is by helping people in our industry with any problems they might have so they can better meet the needs of their customers.

We provide our members with a variety of services. Our website keeps the membership up-to-date on the latest news and trends in the industry. We offer continuing education courses to our members at various venues throughout the country. We have trade meetings in different cities during the year and also put on two major trade shows. We help our members network and we also work with state associations in the industry.

We are very involved in advocacy work for our membership and the industry. That means supporting and recommending legislation on the federal and state level that will help our membership and the industry in general.

One of the most important things we have is a very up-to-date job board, where members can look for employment. We also have space on our website where members can post their résumés and perhaps connect with someone hiring in their area. We work with high schools and colleges to promote our industry to try to bring new blood into our industry's workforce. We also promote the industry to the public.

In addition, we do a great deal of research. We look into safety issues, for instance, as well as the latest materials being used in the industry, gauge what the public wants, check public opinion about the industry and what can be done to keep the industry positive in the public eye.

I oversee all these efforts. It's a massive job that only gets done with an efficient, hardworking staff. Most of the areas like continuing education, advocacy, marketing, and public relations, have individual directors, but before any plan is put into action I have to approve it.

We are governed by an elected board of the dues-paying members. When the board meets, which is on a monthly basis, I go over every program or idea the association is going to implement or is even thinking about for the future. We get the board's input on everything. If board members have any questions, I have to have the answers. So when you are an executive director of an association, you really have to know everything that is going on in the organization.

Members have to feel they are getting their money's worth for their membership dues. You have to try to address a wide range of concerns that members have and you must keep your pulse on the industry at all times. You want to try to be aware of problems in the industry before they are brought to your attention by the membership and be able to address those problems immediately, or at least have several suggestions for solutions.

This is not a typical nine-to-five-type job because there is something going on in the industry all the time and we really have to be on top of it all. Many of our trade shows and meetings, and those being sponsored by statewide associations, take place on the weekends.

The work trade associations do is very important. It gives an industry a voice, it gives people in the industry a place to turn to for advice and guidance, it encourages pride in the business, and it establishes camaraderie in a particular field that keeps the industry strong for generations to come."

PERSONAL QUALIFICATIONS

ALL MANAGERS MUST HAVE A CLEAR vision of what the organization can accomplish and how it can reach its goals. Your resolve is unshakable, your confidence in the organization and its mission unwavering, and you are an irrepressible advocate for the cause. Good leaders inspire everybody around them – staff and volunteers alike.

Spotting talent is one of your key skills. You know a good potential employee when you see one. You hire a dedicated, gifted staff because you know that people are the backbone of the organization and they make it possible to get things done.

Good communications skills are a must. What good is having a clear vision if you cannot communicate all aspects of that vision. Good communications means holding frequent staff meetings, attending regular brainstorming and goal-setting sessions, sending emails and memos, and keeping everybody in the loop all the time. It involves having a crisp, clear writing style and a no-nonsense, straightforward way of speaking.

Listening is important as well. In a management position, people turn to you for ideas all the time. You also know that others – staff, volunteers, the people the nonprofit serves – might have good suggestions as well, and you take the time to listen to their thoughts and see how their ideas can be put into action. You are approachable. People feel comfortable talking to you, expressing their ideas, their concerns, and their problems. The organization thrives on your open-door policy, which you know leads to a more productive workplace.

Boundless energy goes into everything you do and you overlook no detail, no matter how small. You begin each day well prepared and well organized, ready to hit the ground running. Your leadership ability is indisputable and you are able to rally people around you to give a little extra when it is needed most.

Diplomacy is a big part of this job. Those in nonprofit management work with a board of directors, employees, volunteers, and donors all the time. Knowing how to work well with people to reach common ground to fulfill the organization's mission is paramount to the success of the work you are doing. Too much is at stake for personality conflicts to get in the way of reaching your goals.

Conflict resolution is your specialty. Knowing how to resolve conflicts in a sensible, peaceful manner is a must.

Problem solving is another one of your talents. You look for creative ways to overcome any difficulties that might stand in the way of the organization completing its mission.

Those in management project the image of the organization and there is nothing more important than for you to be seen as honest and trustworthy. People want to know that they are donating money to a forthright, sincere group, with leadership that is beyond reproach.

ATTRACTIVE FEATURES

NOTHING GETS YOUR BLOOD FLOWING like being involved in a crusade you truly believe in. Most people do not have as much time as they would like to devote to supporting causes they are passionate about. When you work for a nonprofit, your job is built around the cause, and when you are in management, you are leading that effort.

Most people who work at a nonprofit choose to be there because the organization reflects their personal beliefs and worldview. As a manager for a nonprofit, you are managing people who are already motivated by the cause and want to get things done. Employees at nonprofits are ready and willing all the way to complete a task. What more could people in management want from their workers?

This is a hands-on job, even in management. When you hold a management position at a nonprofit, you do more than sit behind a desk. You get involved in the day-to-day activities in the workplace. At a food pantry, for instance, you might help distribute food; at a homeless shelter, you might give out blankets or serve a hot meal; at a military veterans' organization, you could be needed to help clients fill out forms to get benefits. It is good to spend some time on the front lines because you never lose touch with the people you serve – what they need and the issues your organization addresses. It also gives you a chance to roll up your sleeves and work side by side with your employees and volunteers.

Working in management at a nonprofit, you gain valuable experience juggling tight budgets, where every penny counts. It forces you to be creative, finding ways of meeting the group's needs.

As a nonprofit manager, you do not have to satisfy stockholders only interested in profits, which may come at the expense of people who work for the company or the customers the company serves. At nonprofits, people come first.

UNATTRACTIVE ASPECTS

THE NONPROFIT FIELD IS VERY COMPETITIVE when it comes to fundraising. There are many worthy causes and nobody can contribute to all of them. The competition for donor dollars is fierce, especially since most nonprofits rely on donations just to exist. The fundraising efforts of large, nationally known nonprofits, like the American Red Cross or the American Cancer Society, can easily dwarf the fundraising drives of much smaller local nonprofits. The large, well-known nonprofits also have less difficulty attracting donors with deep pockets.

This can be frustrating for the managers of small to medium-sized nonprofits, because those organizations may not enjoy the same name recognition as the ones with a regional or national profile. In a leadership role at a nonprofit, you might find that you are putting more time and effort into fundraising than you would like, but that is the lifeblood of a nonprofit. Fundraising is a constant, even overriding, concern because the amount of money that can be raised from year to year is always unpredictable.

As a nonprofit manager, you put in long hours, sometimes on weekends and holidays, depending on the services the organization provides and events that may be scheduled. Usually, nonprofits do not pay overtime. So while some major nonprofits can offer salaries competitive with those in the corporate sector, most smaller organizations cannot. That is why people who go into nonprofit work have to be dedicated to the cause and the job and not in it for the money.

No matter how much you would like to help everybody who comes to you for assistance, you rarely can. Most nonprofits have rules. There may be limits on how much you can do for a person or a family. The organization may only be able to help people who live in a certain area or who meet specific income requirements. Your nonprofit could have funding to pay for heating for low-income senior citizens, but have no money to fix broken windows that may be letting cold air into that same home.

As well-meaning as you are, you are going to have failures and they hurt. When you work for a nonprofit advocacy group, it can be exasperating waiting for government officials to take action to pass legislation changing how things are done. It can be infuriating when it takes legislators years to vote on commonsense legislation to protect woodlands, streams, and lakes, or to safeguard animal rights. The delay creates a backlog in other advocacy work you want to do and other legislation your organization would like to see passed. That also hinders your ability to show donors that something has been accomplished.

Because nonprofits are on a tight budget, you probably will not be working with the latest technology or have the most modern office.

Limited staff is another problem caused by limited resources. That means fewer people have to take on more responsibility. When you have a limited staff, and they have to work very hard to meet your organization's goals, you run the risk of having employees burn out and leave their jobs.

EDUCATION AND TRAINING

MANY OF THE SKILLS LEARNED WHEN getting a college degree in business administration can be applied to running a nonprofit organization, but there are some elements of a nonprofit, such as working with volunteers, forging ties with community activists, and raising money through appeals, that are not addressed in a business administration major. That is why numerous colleges now have programs specially designed for students who want to go into a career in nonprofit management, and the list of colleges with those programs is growing all the time.

Arizona State University in Phoenix offers a bachelor's degree in nonprofit leadership and management through its Lodestar Center for Philanthropy & Nonprofit Innovation. Courses cover a wide range of subjects, including an Introduction to Nonprofits, Volunteer Management, Fundraising and Resource Development, Leadership, Nonprofit Marketing, and Grant Writing, among others. The school also offers a master's degree in nonprofit leadership and management.

Students at Indiana University in Bloomington can major in public and nonprofit management at the university's School of Public and Environmental Affairs. Students can choose either a public management or a nonprofit management track. In the nonprofit track, students take courses in Nonprofit Management and Leadership, Fund Development for Nonprofits, Nonprofits and the Voluntary Sector, Public Relations for Nonprofits, and Program Evaluation.

Indiana University offers students the opportunity to major in a variety of other subjects, like environmental science, and minor in nonprofit management. School administrators believe that offering nonprofit management as a minor gives students the chance to expand their horizons when looking for employment.

Nonprofit and Social Innovations is one of the tracks students can embark on when getting a Bachelor of Science degree in policy, planning, and development at the University of Southern California (USC). The program is offered at the university's Sol Price School of Public Policy in Sacramento. The program has courses on the Nonprofit Sector and the Public Interest, Management of Public and Nonprofit Organizations, Public Service in an Urban Setting, and Social Innovations. Students at USC can also minor in nonprofits, philanthropy, and volunteerism.

The Bachelor of Arts degree in nonprofit leadership at LaGrange College in Georgia is geared to training people to handle management positions at any type of nonprofit organization. Critical thinking, leadership skills, and communication techniques are the building blocks of this program, which also features an internship.

The bachelor's degree in nonprofit administration at Cleveland State University in Ohio has a focus on urban nonprofits. Contemporary Urban Issues as well as Urban Policy are two of the program's required courses. Other courses include Management of Urban and Nonprofit Organizations, Proposal Writing, Organizational Behavior, Neighborhood Planning, and Social Welfare Policy. Cleveland State University offers a master's degree in public administration with a specialization in nonprofit management, as well as a master's in nonprofit administration and leadership.

To earn an undergraduate degree in nonprofit management at North Park University in Chicago, students have to complete an internship. In addition, students take classes in Nonprofit Governance and Volunteer Management, Advanced Nonprofit Marketing and Fundraising, Nonprofit Management Economics, and other related classes.

Organizational development, strategic planning, human resource management, and financial management are the underpinnings of the major in management of nonprofit organizations at Johnson University in Knoxville, Tennessee. An internship with a nonprofit organization is also part of the program.

Larger nonprofits often look for management personnel who have a master's degree in nonprofit management, so some colleges and universities offer those advanced degrees. People working in the nonprofit sector can start out in the field after getting their bachelor's degree and earn their master's degree part time while working at their first job.

Some schools prefer those applying for their master's degree program to have a particular type of undergraduate degree, such as a bachelor's degree in business administration. So if you are thinking of pursuing a master's in nonprofit management, it is a good idea to plan ahead and check with the schools you would like to attend for your advanced degree. Ask the admissions officers which undergraduate degree their school would consider desirable for somebody looking to get into the nonprofit management master's program.

Schools offering advanced degrees in nonprofit management include the University of Notre Dame in Indiana; Worcester State University in Massachusetts; Washington University in St. Louis; Regis University in Denver; the University of Georgia in Athens, Georgia; the University of Pennsylvania in Philadelphia; the University of Wisconsin-Milwaukee; Fordham University in New York City; the University of San Diego; and the University of Oregon in Eugene, Oregon.

Because of the vast range of nonprofits and their different missions, most schools design their programs with a particular emphasis, providing their students with a unique perspective on the field. It is worth taking the time to look into a number of schools when seeking an advanced degree in nonprofit management and find the program that best suits your professional goals.

EARNINGS

THERE ARE SO MANY DIFFERENT TYPES of nonprofit organizations that no general statement can be made about salaries for all of them. When people hear "nonprofit," they often think low paychecks, but that is not always the case.

Some big nonprofits, like educational institutions, trade associations, and national advocacy groups, offer their management personnel salaries that are comparable to those in the corporate world. Compensation usually depends on how much money a nonprofit is able to bring in through donations and grants.

Those who choose a career in management at nonprofits usually move around quite a bit in their careers until they land a job at a salary they are happy with. At small nonprofits that have an annual revenue of $500,000 to $1 million, an executive director might command an annual salary in the $45,000 to $60,000 range. Managers in fundraising and programs earn a bit less, usually between $35,000 and $55,000.

At medium-sized nonprofits with yearly budgets in the $1 million to $5 million range, executive directors earn between $75,000 and $90,000 annually. The pay scale for directors of fundraising, community outreach, special events, and volunteers is in the $60,000 to $85,000 bracket.

Nonprofits with $5 million to $10 million in annual revenues pay their executive directors between $100,000 and $150,000, and possibly more. The salary of a particular executive director depends on how long that person has been with the organization. Directors of other departments, like fundraising, can earn between $90,000 and $125,000.

A nonprofit with an annual budget of $10 million-plus may employ an executive director with a salary over $250,000, and directors of particular departments earn well over $100,000 each.

OPPORTUNITIES

JOB GROWTH IN THE NONPROFIT SECTOR is projected to outpace that in the corporate world by 15 percent, according to a recently released Nonprofit Employment Practices Survey. A broad cross section of hundreds of nonprofits nationwide participated in the survey. The report is intended to give a snapshot of the latest hiring trends in the nonprofit sector.

According to the report, 50 percent of the nonprofits surveyed are planning to increase staff over the next few years, while only 36 percent of for-profit corporations surveyed are planning on new hiring. The survey shows that nonprofits are continuing to rebound from the Great Recession and now have a total workforce of 10.7 million people throughout the nation. The nonprofit sector is the third-largest employer in the country. To meet their various missions, nonprofits collectively raise more than $1.9 trillion annually.

An interesting note in the survey is that 91 percent of the organizations participating in the study reported using contacts made through networking to identify people to hire when looking to increase staff or fill vacant jobs.

Of course, not all the new hiring by nonprofits will be in management, but employment in management positions in nonprofits is expected to grow by at least 12 percent in the next decade. Part of that projected growth is attributed to nonprofits adding additional services over the next few decades for aging baby boomers, and the need for people in management to oversee those programs.

In addition, many nonprofits are starting to pick up more of the slack as government agencies on all levels cut or eliminate a variety of social and human services. This increases the need for nonprofit managers.

Some of the largest projected job growth in the nonprofit sector is in faith-based groups as well as in organizations involved with social and human services, healthcare, the environment, animal welfare, education, and research. Besides executive directors, the biggest areas of job growth in nonprofit management are expected to be among those who oversee direct services, programs, fundraising, community outreach, and member services.

The number of new nonprofits in the nation continues to grow as successful entrepreneurs, especially in high-tech fields, plow some of their profits into organizations that address social ills, not only in this nation but worldwide. This creates new opportunities for people who want to work in the nonprofit sector, especially in management. In addition, some of the nonprofits founded since the last quarter of the 20th century have turned into powerhouses. These include Susan G. Komen for the Cure, Teach for America, Make-A-Wish Foundation, American Kidney Fund, and Habitat for Humanity. As these types of nonprofits grow, so does the need for training people for management jobs in these organizations.

Over 200 nonprofits, excluding hospitals and universities, started after 1975, have now eclipsed the $50 million mark in annual revenues. As these big nonprofits expand and open local and regional offices to provide services on the grassroots level, more professional managers will be employed.

GETTING STARTED

MOST NONPROFITS OFFER INTERNSHIPS, and these internships are an excellent way to learn what it is like to work for a nonprofit. Even a nonpaying internship is worth taking, for the insights and experience you will gain. As an intern, you get an insider's view of the problems, tough choices, decision-making policy, and rewards that go with the job. You will also get a behind-the-scenes look at the day-to-day operation of the nonprofit and see the commitment it takes to run one of these organizations.

This is a field where you have to do your research to find a job at a nonprofit that is right for you. Make a list of nonprofits you think you would like to work for and look into each one. There are plenty of online sources of information about nonprofits. GuideStar, for instance, is a website devoted to gathering and disseminating information about every IRS-registered nonprofit in the nation. The site has data on each nonprofit's mission, programs, finances, budget, reputation, and a variety of other important facts.

Look for news articles about a nonprofit where you are thinking of working and perhaps even attend one of its events. Talk to the people at the event. Try to get a feel for the organization and the people who support it. Gauge the commitment of the people who are involved with this nonprofit. Find out as much as you can about a nonprofit before going there for a job interview. This way you can ask questions about the organization to determine if this is a job where you will be happy.

While the largest nonprofits have the biggest budgets, few nonprofit managers begin their careers at the biggest and most prominent nonprofits. Most people entering the nonprofit sector find their first jobs at small to medium-sized organizations. That is a good place to start because you learn a lot and gain some valuable experience. The smaller the nonprofit, the more responsibility you have, and that enables people in management to learn the ins and outs of the nonprofit world. When larger nonprofits look for management personnel, they usually turn to people who have a proven track record with a small to mid-sized nonprofit.

Nonprofits are a tight-knit community, sharing the same concerns and problems. You will be able to start networking early in your career, making contacts with people you will work with and turn to for advice throughout your working days in the nonprofit sector. Take the time to develop these contacts. They will help you succeed and advance in this field.

ASSOCIATIONS

■ **National Council of Nonprofits**
www.councilofnonprofits.org

■ **Society for Nonprofits**
www.snpo.org/index.php

■ **Alliance for Nonprofit Management**
https://allianceonline.org

■ **Association of Fundraising Professionals (AFP)**
http://www.afpnet.org

■ **Council on Foundations**
http://www.cof.org

■ **Young Nonprofit Professional Network (YNPN)**
http://www.ynpn.org

■ **American Society of Association Executives (ASAE)**
http://www.asaecenter.org

WEBSITES

■ **Alliance for Nonprofit Excellence**
http://www.npexcellence.org

■ **Nonprofit Leadership Alliance**
www.nonprofitleadershipalliance.org

■ **GuideStar**
http://www.guidestar.org

■ **Nonprofit Expert**
www.nonprofitexpert.com

■ **Foundation Center**
http://foundationcenter.org

■ **Nonprofit Tech for Good**
http://www.nptechforgood.com

■ **Idealist**
http://www.idealist.org

■ **GrantSpace**
http://grantspace.org

■ **Center for Nonprofit Advancement**
https://www.nonprofitadvancement.org

■ **Bridgespan**
http://www.bridgespan.org

■ **CompassPoint**
https://www.compasspoint.org

■ **Grassroots.org**
http://www.grassroots.org

■ **Partnership in Philanthropy Support Center**
http://supportcenteronline.org

www.ingramcontent.com/pod-product-compliance
Lightning Source LLC
Chambersburg PA
CBHW070426190526
45169CB00003B/1432